Volcanoes

Maria Gordon

Cavendish
Square

New York

Published in 2014 by Cavendish Square Publishing, LLC
303 Park Avenue South, Suite 1247, New York, NY 10010
Copyright © 2014 by Cavendish Square Publishing, LLC

First Edition

CPSIA Compliance Information: Batch #WW14CSQ

All websites were available and accurate when this book was sent to press.

Library of Congress Cataloging-in-Publication Data
Gordon, Maria.
Volcanoes / by Maria Gordon.
p. cm. — (Surprising science)
Includes index.
ISBN 978-1-62712-319-8 (hardcover)
ISBN 978-1-62712-320-4 (paperback)
ISBN 978-1-62712-321-1 (ebook)
1. Volcanoes — Juvenile literature. I. Title.
QE522.G67 2014
551.21—dc23

Printed in the United States of America

The photographs in this book are used by permission and through the courtesy of: Cover photo by © Rainer Albiez/Shutterstock.com; © Rainer Albiez/Shutterstock.com, 1; © Catmando/Shutterstock.com, 3; © beboy/Shutterstock.com, 4; © Photovolcanica.com/Shutterstock.com, 5; © Laurin Rinder/Shutterstock.com, 6; Gringer/Pacific Ring of Fire/vector data from CIA World DataBank II, 7; © wdeon/Shutterstock.com, 8; © Byelikova Oksana/Shutterstock.com, 8; © Dariush M/Shutterstock.com, 9; © Dr. Morley Read/Shutterstock.com, 10; NASA, modifications by Seddon/Olympus Mons alt/nssdc.gsfc.nasa.gov/photo_gallery_photogallery-mars.html#features, 11; © Ammit Jack/Shutterstock.com, 12; © James R. Hearn/Shutterstock.com, 12; © Catmando/Shutterstock.com, 13; © Steve Bower/Shutterstock.com, 14; © Ammit Jack/Shutterstock.com, 14; FujiSunriseKawaguchiko2025WP, 14; Willie Scott, USGS/MSH06 aerial crater from north high angle 09-12-06/vulcan.wr.usgs.gov/Volcanoes/MSH/Images/MSH04/crater_dome_eruption_september_2006.html, 14; © Siim Sepp/Shutterstock.com, 15; Howell Williams/NOAA, 16; es0teric/Mount Erebus 6/Flickr/Creative Commons Attribution-Share Alike 2.0 Generic license, 17; © bierchen/Shutterstock.com, 18; © RZ Design/Shutterstock.com, 18; © Warren Goldswain/Shutterstock.com, 19; © Bychkov Kirill/Shutterstock.com, 20; Forest and Kim Starr/Starr 060228-8947 Aerial photograph of Hawaii/Plants of Hawaii, Image 060228-8947/Creative Commons Attribution 3.0 Unported license, 21.

Editorial Director: Dean Miller
Art Director: Jeffrey Talbot

Content and Design by quadrum™
www.quadrumltd.com

Volcanoes

CHAPTER 1

The word volcano gets its name from the Roman god of fire, Vulcan.

Eruptions

About 1,500 volcanoes have erupted in the past 10,000 years. At any given time, about twenty volcanoes are erupting.

Have you heard of erupting mountains? These landforms are not mountains, they are known as volcanoes. A volcano is a landform through which hot **molten** liquid **erupts**. Even though it looks a lot like a large mountain, it is very different in nature. Volcanoes are formed when hot molten liquid from inside Earth rises to the surface through cracks in its **crust**.

Not all volcanoes erupt. An active volcano erupts often. A **dormant** volcano does not erupt often but may erupt again. An extinct volcano is one that has not erupted for at least 10,000 years and is not expected to erupt ever again.

The largest volcano on Earth is Mauna Loa in Hawaii. Its height measures more than 10.5 miles!

The hot molten liquid under Earth's surface is known as magma. As pressure in the molten rock builds, the magma needs to escape. So it forces its way up **fissures**, which are narrow cracks in Earth's crust. Once this magma erupts through Earth's surface, it is called lava.

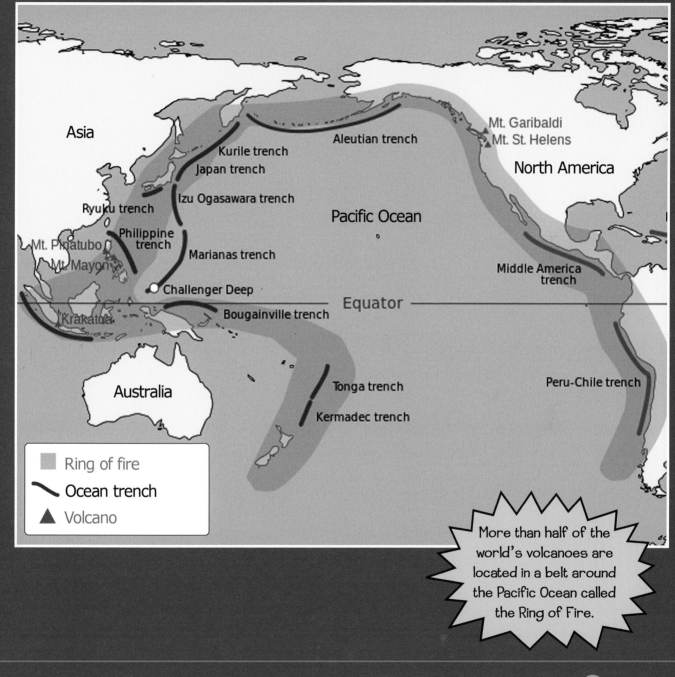

Asia

Kurile trench

Japan trench

Izu Ogasawara trench

Ryuku trench

Philippine trench

Mt. Pinatubo

Mt. Mayon

Marianas trench

Challenger Deep

Krakatoa

Bougainville trench

Australia

Aleutian trench

Mt. Garibaldi
Mt. St. Helens

North America

Pacific Ocean

Equator

Middle America trench

Tonga trench

Kermadec trench

Peru-Chile trench

Ring of fire

Ocean trench

▲ Volcano

More than half of the world's volcanoes are located in a belt around the Pacific Ocean called the Ring of Fire.

CHAPTER 2

The most dangerous volcano on Earth is Popocatepetl, also known as "El Popo." It is just thirty-three miles from Mexico City. El Popo is a violent volcano that emits tons of gas and ash into the air every year.

Why Do They Erupt?

To understand volcanoes, you need to first understand Earth's **geology**. Volcanoes generally exist along the edges between tectonic plates, which are massive rock slabs that make up the Earth's surface. Earth has three main layers: the crust, the mantle, and the core. The crust is made up of solid rock and varies in thickness.

The mantle is a thick layer of molten rock called magma, and the core is made up of a solid center covered by an outer layer of liquid.

There are about 6,000 active volcanoes under water. That's four times the number of active volcanoes on land!

The farthest point from the center of Earth is the summit of the volcano Chimborazo in Ecuador.

Earth's crust is made up of huge rock slabs called tectonic plates, which fit together like a jigsaw puzzle. These plates often move. When this happens, a section of one plate slides over the other. The magma gets squeezed between these plates, causing it to erupt.

Volcanoes are not just on Earth—the biggest known volcano in our solar system is on Mars. It is known as Olympus Mons, and is 373 miles wide and 13 miles high!

CHAPTER 3

One of the most **destructive** recent eruptions was in Mount St. Helens in the state of Washington in 1980. The volcano exploded with **fury**, destroying more than 250 homes, 47 bridges, and 185 miles of highway.

Varied Volcanoes

Electricity can be generated from the heat emitted by volcanoes. The electricity that is **extracted** from volcanoes is known as geothermal energy. Cold water is pumped down to the rocks, which heat the water and turn it into steam. This steam is then piped to a power plant to make electricity.

Most people think of volcanoes as large, cone-shaped mountains, but that is just one type. Others resemble wide plateaus and bulging domes. Some very important volcanoes do not look like mountains at all. They look like deep lakes because they have had huge eruptions that caused the ground to sag.

Scientists have divided volcanoes into four different types: shield, cinder cone, composite, and lava dome.

Shield Volcano

Cinder Cone Volcano

Composite Volcano

Lava Dome Volcano

As the volcano continues to erupt, the lava flows out and settles on its slopes. Over time, it cools down and turns to firm rock. This is how a volcano gets bigger and bigger.

Shield volcanoes have dull, broad slopes. They are generally shaped like a bowl, with a shield in the middle and long slopes that are created due to lava flows. Cinder cones are circular or oval in shape and made up of small lava particles. Composite volcanoes are **precipitous** and composed of several layers of volcanic rock. Lava domes are molded by the erupting lava that is too heavy to flow, creating a mountain as the lava piles up.

Surtsey is an island that has formed at the southernmost point of Iceland. It is a result of an active underwater volcano. This new island popped up in the ocean on November 14, 1963. Since then, it has considerably increased and decreased in size depending on the volcanic activity under water!

There are more active volcanoes on the ocean beds than on land! Every day, somewhere on Earth, a volcano erupts. Fortunately, most of the volcanic eruptions are under water. There are about 6,000 active underwater volcanoes, also known as seamounts. Smaller submarine volcanoes are called sea knolls. Flat-topped seamounts are called guyots. Sometimes, the lava from seamounts forms islands.

The southernmost active volcano on Earth is Mount Erebus. This volcano has been active for a very long time even though it is found in Antarctica and covered in ice!

17

CHAPTER 4

18

The sound of a volcanic eruption can be soft or explosive. Loud, explosive sounds can travel hundreds of miles!

Vicious Volcanoes

When volcanoes are active, they often release ash, gas, and hot magma in violent yet **spectacular** eruptions. The danger zone around a volcano covers about a twenty-mile radius. Eruptions can cause lava flows, hot ash flows, mudslides, avalanches, falling ash, and lava floods.

Sometimes, there are massive volcanic explosions due to the rapid expansion of gases. One such example is the island of Krakatoa. In 1883, a volcano exploded on the island and completely destroyed it, leaving nothing but ocean behind!

Volcanic eruptions can cause ash to spew into the air at heights greater than seventeen miles above Earth's surface.

Volcanic reactions can be very harmful at times. Fresh volcanic ash, made of **pulverized** rock, can be harsh, acidic, and smelly. The ash can drastically damage your lungs. An erupting volcano can trigger other natural disasters, such as tsunamis, flash floods, earthquakes, mudflows, and rockfalls.

However, Earth would be very different without volcanoes. Gaseous **emissions** from volcanoes formed the Earth's atmosphere. The sea floor and some mountains were formed by countless volcanic eruptions.

It is estimated that around 80 percent of the Earth's surface, above and below sea level, has originated due to volcanic activity. The magma, molten rock, and debris from volcanic eruptions have created some major landforms such as islands, mountains, plateaus, and plains.

Glossary

crust [KRUST] the outer most layer of Earth's surface

destructive [de-STRUK-tive] a tendency to hurt or destroy

dormant [DOOR-mant] to be inactive

emissions [e-MIS-shens] gaseous substances given off in the air

erupt [ir-RUPT] to burst or explode due to limits or restraint

extracted [ex-TRACT-ed] squeezed out or removed

fissures [FISH-erz] a narrow opening, crack or slit

fury [FYU-ree] destructive rage

geology [gee-ALL-o-gee] the rocks, land, and processes of land formation

molten [MOLE-tin] a substance that is liquefied by heat

precipitous [pre-SIP-uh-tes] very steep

pulverized [PUL-ver-eyes] to be crushed or beaten

spectacular [spek-TAK-ku-lar] something that is amazing

Books to Discover

Adams, Simon. *The Best Book of Volcanoes*. London: Kingfisher Publications, 2007.

Schreiber, Anne. *National Geographic Kids: Volcanoes*. Washington DC: National Geographic Society, 2008.

Ganeri, Anita. *Eruption! The Story of Volcanoes*. New York: DK Publishing, 2010.

Websites to Explore

Encyclopedia Britannica
www.britannica.com/EBchecked/topic/632130/volcano

How Stuff Works
www.howstuffworks.com/nature/natural-disasters/volcano.htm

National Geographic
environment.nationalgeographic.com/environment/natural-disasters/volcano-profile/

A Quiz about Volcanoes
kids.nationalgeographic.com/kids/games/puzzlesquizzes/quizyournoodle-volcanoes/

Index

Page numbers in **boldface** are images.